Parking Meters into Mermaids

poems by

Merrill Oliver Douglas

Finishing Line Press
Georgetown, Kentucky

Parking Meters
into Mermaids

Copyright © 2020 by Merrill Oliver Douglas
ISBN 978-1-64662-313-6 First Edition
All rights reserved under International and Pan-American Copyright Conventions. No part of this book may be reproduced in any manner whatsoever without written permission from the publisher, except in the case of brief quotations embodied in critical articles and reviews.

ACKNOWLEDGMENTS

Many thanks to the journals in which the following poems originally appeared, some in slightly different form:

A Narrow Fellow, "While Our Mothers Talked and Smoked" and "Lullaby"
Baltimore Review, "Summer, In My Early Twenties"
Cimarron Review, "The Women Who Came Before Me"
Connotation Press: An Online Artifact, "Raccoons in the Attic"
Crab Creek Review, "Allied Maintenance"
Eunoia Review, "What the Dream Reveals About Her Father"
Lips, "Mirrors, Eyes"
Persimmon Tree, "Bathhouse, Brighton Beach, 1958"
Paterson Literary Review, "Savor"
San Pedro River Review, "The Distance from There to Here"
South 85 Journal, "Bereft"
Sugar House Review, "Harvest" and "Flight"

Publisher: Leah Maines
Editor: Christen Kincaid
Cover Art: Jamie Douglas, http://www.jamie-douglas.com/
Author Photo: Edwin Douglas
Cover Design: Elizabeth Maines McCleavy

Printed in the USA on acid-free paper.
Order online: www.finishinglinepress.com
 also available on amazon.com

Author inquiries and mail orders:
Finishing Line Press
P. O. Box 1626
Georgetown, Kentucky 40324
U. S. A.

Table of Contents

Flight 1
The Women Who Came Before Me 2
Bathhouse, Brighton Beach, 1958 3
Mirrors, Eyes 4
While Our Mothers Talked and Smoked 5
No Training Wheels 6
When We Weren't Fighting 7
Skelly 8
Raccoons in the Attic 9
Volunteer 10
Eleventh Grade 11
Summer, in My Early Twenties 12
1978 13
Allied Maintenance 14
What the Dream Reveals About Her Father 15
Lullaby 16
The Distance from There to Here 17
End of Summer 18
Going There 19
Bargaining 20
Savor 21
After 22
Stuff 23
I Take Up Yarn Bombing 25
Bereft 26
Aubade 27
Living 28
Harvest 30

Flight

The ten-year-old finds a wing suit
like the one she saw on TV,
but in her own size,
squirrel membranes fanned
from arm to hip. In her mind
she's zipped it on already
and gone gliding from roof to roof
in that spiked, glass-glittering city
she loves with a serenity
she'll never feel, when grown,
for husband, friend or child.

In our first year, the man
I would one day marry
told me that given a chance
to help settle another world—
a one-way voyage, of course,
with no certainty he'd land alive—
he'd grab it, no question
or need to ask anyone's blessing.
And there I'd be, barefoot
in the dry grass, watering tomatoes,
watching the sun set and rise.

The Women Who Came Before Me

They buttoned their thick tweed coats to the chin
and nagged their kids to tug knit hats low on their ears until April.
They knew the price, to the cent, of canned peas at each of three
    markets.
On Sundays they'd sit face to face in the kitchen, slapping down
    coupons
like aces and jacks, swapping stories about Manya and Sonya
and Selma, and Abe from downstairs. They boiled the orange out of
    carrots,
tucked a cooked egg in the meatloaf, swore by Tab and Melba Toast.
They scrubbed the linoleum spotless but never walked if they could
    catch a ride,
never got wet without bathing caps, never went barefoot.
All these years I've been trying to outgrow those dresses they
    shortened
to fit me, working on their knees, mouths bristling with straight pins.

Bathhouse, Brighton Beach, 1958

The way my grandmother's belly sagged
when she peeled her swim suit off
her shoulders, over hips and knees,
confused me: that pale flesh looked so much
like a second, smaller pair of breasts.
But what made a navel grow there?
Or could that pinched-in spot be a secret
extra eye that studied me
watching her towel her thighs
and bottom and smooth on powder
like lilacs blooming in bunches
over the fish-cold cement floor?

Mirrors, Eyes

My grandfather takes off his glasses.
Who is this stranger? I won't go near him,
not even when he makes the Donald Duck voice.

I get measles and cry
at the sight of my own face.
My mother hangs a blanket on the mirror.
Five days I lie in bed, lights off,
shades drawn, radio glowing.

They cover mirrors, too,
when my grandfather dies. It's the custom.
Bathroom, bedroom, wherever you go
there's a bedsheet or towel.

In a few weeks, people
stop saying his name.
He's gone like steam from the glass,

except for one framed photo.
My sister and I wear straw hats.
Poppy smiles behind us,
a hand on each girl's shoulder.

I don't let my eyes meet his,
and I turn away fast.

While Our Mothers Talked and Smoked

In the bushes near the iron fence
we'd sometimes find a bottle,
contents drained, but around the lip
a brown crust of sharp-scented sugar
we'd pick off and sniff on our fingers.

I knew those bottles came from men
called bums, whom I'd spot here and there
on the benches, turned round
the wrong way, knees wedged
into the space between seat and back rest.

No one's neighbors, no one's uncles,
they lay their foreheads on crossed arms,
bellies lifting and falling,
as fiercely asleep as our brothers
and sisters tipped back in their strollers,

plastic nipples loosed from the babies'
slack mouths trailing glints of milk.

No Training Wheels

Early Sunday, my father and I walk my bike to the courthouse.
He steadies the frame while I boost myself to the seat
and then he jogs, one hand on the back wheel's fender.
Squares of empty plaza slip beneath us, faster and faster.

Suddenly he's out front (*this is impossible!*) soft-shoeing
backwards, tongue loose, fingers wriggling near his ears like bugs.
I start to scream.

                But I know how this works:
all my life I've been watching that coyote in the cartoons.
Legs in a whirr, he shoots off the cliff and keeps wheeling straight
across a void that holds as long as he doesn't look down. So I don't.

When We Weren't Fighting

Some mornings I'd curl
knees to chest on my bed
while my sister heaped
comforter and plaid spread
on top, then dragged

the matching blanket
and spread from her own
twin bed to pile on, too.
She'd plump her pillow
on mine, climb up.

Who did she think she was
balanced there—
princess in a tower?
Lindsey Nelson calling balls
and strikes for the Mets?

Burrowed in the
mouse-scent of my
own skin and sleep, how
quickly I felt her slight weight
wink out: trivial rumor.

Skelly*

Everyone knew how to pack
crushed crayon stubs in bottle caps
and float those caps on hot water
to make the wax melt slowly.

Downstairs, we flicked them
from chalked square to square,
1 to 13, until someone turned
Killer and blasted the others away.

But first came the patient art:
playing the stove's flame
to trouble the water just short
of boiling, the soft crumbs

of Yellow and Scarlet,
or Aquamarine and Cobalt
undoing themselves
without pain, the way I'd like

to think the soul—
which I believe in only
when I hold my breath—
lets go at last, and then cools.

*Skelly: An urban game played on the sidewalk, using weighted bottle caps. Also called skully, skelsies and other names.

Raccoons in the Attic

When I hear them thumping over loose planks
and gnawing at the wood in the kitchen soffits,
I think of that man and woman and their boy

who lived upstairs from us in Queens. We rarely saw them
face to face, but their steps in our ceiling belonged to the everyday
weather of home, like fish frying, or flies at the window.

Their shoes clapped back and forth on wood parquet like ours,
in a living room exactly like ours, same late day sun
on the sill, same view of playground, school and mall.

The father used to yell in swollen baritone waves
we assumed were Italian: as hard as I eavesdropped
I couldn't have imagined what he wanted, any more

than I can think my way into the muscles
of sharp-toothed animals settling their bodies into pink insulation
on a frozen morning, nothing between us but Sheetrock.

Volunteer

A blond, brain-injured child in shorts, with hard knees,
Henry could walk but spoke only in vowels.
Every four hours, one of the parents stretched him face down
on a table to push through the motions of creeping.

Patterning, they called it: exercise to build
the brain by way of muscles. They lent us a book.
Scientists called this a quack cure,
but Linda and I were sixteen and just wanted to help.

The father moved the right limbs, Linda the head,
and I worked the left. Like dancing a frog.
Sometimes he let us. Sometimes he'd twist and whine
and we had to beg: *Don't make us get out the strap!*

But at some point every week I stood squeezing and
squeezing my fists while the father whipped
and the boy went rigid, snot in strings down his chin.

Later, we'd smear peanut butter down the gums
and into the palate to make the tongue work hard.
That smell—oil, salt, spit—that paste on my finger:

decades later, whenever I use a wet dish rag to dig
the last smudge of Jif from a jar, it disgusts me.

Eleventh Grade

My friend built a scarecrow
dressed in a plaid shirt and straw hat,
Halloween mask for a face.
He named it Angus, propped it to sit
on a straight-backed chair in his bedroom,
settled a cracked guitar in its arms,
ran the tube of a fish tank pump through
the mouth to a pipe, which he lit.

Angus played me "Bitches Brew,"
Andrés Segovia, bluegrass, The Byrds.
He had no inconvenient girlfriends,
never took off for weeks thumbing rides,
beard grown so full he passed for eighteen.
I could stuff the pipe with tobacco,
weed or ripped chemistry notes
and it made no difference: Angus was pleased.

Summer, in My Early Twenties

Those weeks when the fan on the windowsill
mumbled apologies hour after hour,
I would wake up three or four times a night

and stand at the refrigerator
gulping cold water. Nobody told me
the taste on the mouth of the jar was just

rust from the lid: I was so sure
it was the kiss of disappointment.
Often, it was hard to tell the clutter

in my bedroom from the clutter in my brain,
loose stacks of magazines and notebooks,
postcards, paperbacks, all mixed up

with the name of some man who might
fly back from Costa Rica
or Nepal and hold still long enough to love me.

Nights when the t-shirt stuck to my back,
and I could feel the hairs sprout on my legs,
why didn't some grayer, fatter woman

sit me down and say, "Sweetie, this isn't your life.
This is weather." Maybe I did see the Empire
State Building's head on fire in a fog,

but by morning I would find it had cooled
to a blue coal, the streets all healed. Down the block,
the Italian ice guys would be lifting their garage door,

leading their carts out like ponies,
hosing them down, suds sliding in sheets
across the sidewalk and over the curb's lip.

1978

I never used makeup. I wore a braid
or twisted my hair in a knot.
In summer, an Indian skirt
fit well with a tank top
and canvas sandals I bought
at Woolworth's for $3.99.

I left my legs alone: this was
earthy, feminist, real.
Then one day, walking to work
from the subway, I felt a man
roping my calves
with a long, sweaty stare,

and he called out, *Mmm-mmm!*
I love hairy legs!
That night, I shaved:
it was hard enough
filling the space I took
on this planet as though I deserved it.

Allied Maintenance

When Ed worked third shift,
the best job was strolling the buildings
replacing dead lightbulbs.
Worst was the treater tower,
seven stories high, where lengths
of glass cloth, soaked in epoxy,
rolled past blasts of hot air. First
they pulled the blowers out:
then twenty or thirty guys
climbed the staircase that spiraled
the tower, and stood in the gaps. For hours
they scraped at gobs of dripped resin.

Sometimes the crew spent half the night
hiding. Ed napped in some engineer's chair
or made slow tours of the corridors,
ears alert for supervisors' boots, while Jeff Barr
cracked the day crew's combination locks, for fun.

If I'd been there, I'd have stuck
to my scrubbing, grousing the whole eight hours,
then gone home and switched off the lights,
aware I'd wake soon to the banging of trash cans,
or maybe to Ralph, the landlord's kid,
that basketball slapping a path
down the driveway, morning after morning.

On 2 a.m. lunch breaks the game wasn't poker
or blackjack, as I'd have guessed, but bridge.
Ed had the knack: he thought three moves ahead
and always knew which cards were still in play.

What the Dream Reveals About Her Father

1

The funeral? It was a hoax.
He's lived for years in this walkup,

dishes washed,
shelves stacked with soup cans.

There's no young wife, no collection
of semi-skilled, half-finished paintings,

just this day bed, a TV.
Each morning he chooses a clean shirt,

takes the "F" downtown,
works, rides back.

2

He stands at the window,
forehead to glass

such a long time,
maybe he's dozed off.

But just as I start
toward the door, he turns:

Listen. I'm fine.
They give plenty of heat.

No leaks. No roaches.
And where did you ever

see walls this thick?
(He knocks.) *I swear*

I haven't heard another
human voice in years.

Lullaby

My mother swears by a relentless
jiggling she says bores infants to sleep,
but you're so furious, nothing stops you

who've never heard of first shift
or your father's alarm. At night
when I slip in to undress

I hear him twisting,
twisting in the damp sheets.
You're hardly his son now,
just a loud neighbor. The radio's

seething, I lift you, we're sticky
and slick as I stamp from couch
to table to couch. You're red
as this morning's sunrise, and tomorrow's.

My palm cups your head, we're both crying,
I'm jumping in place, hissing Stop please
please stop it! And bouncing higher
and landing so hard the lamps rattle.

The Distance from There to Here

A kayak is no more than a skin
worn to sit on water.

Seneca Lake is forty miles long
and my son is a bean in a thin pod.

The wind blows the wrong way:
the broad surface darkens.

I brace my feet and haul
hard on the paddle with cold hands.

The boy is a thistle seed
and the lake's iron mouth pulls wide.

Waves shove me north.

End of Summer

It's an old game I play
with my niece's toddler,
on patchy grass
behind Bill's Kitchen.

We're giving his parents
some time alone
with their burgers and fries.
The grass is thick with rocks.

We take turns choosing—
cracked disks, rounded wedges—
fitting them belly to hip
on my takeout container.

Quickly, the flat white
surface fills with decisions,
the kind you can take back:
flip the box, start over.

Child and woman
sorting the earth's bones
under a sky like a lens
the sun squints through.

Going There

I visit the campus
web cam once or twice daily.
I won't see my son: I just want to check
on the air he inhales, sneak
a look at snow or sun whitening the paths
in that place where he walks.

**

Google sets me down on Herzl Street,
exactly the spot where I see my dad lifting
this toddler who grew to be me. A slight screen-
twist brings up the same brick, two-story
houses that rise at our backs in the photo,
as if I could step through glass
into black-and-white Brooklyn
and nuzzle that young man—thirty-five or so
that day, just a few years more than the girl
will have lived when the stroke knocks him dead.

**

Those videos the terrorists post—
no sane mother would watch.
But at night, awake on her back,
she hears blank screens taunt
from all over the house:
*Switch on the power. You need
to feel blade touch neck.*

Bargaining

Slipping out early
for the long drive home,
I don't want breakfast—

just tea. But when my mother
comes from bed, hair still in a net,
to wish me a safe trip, I know

how she'll quiz me:
What did you eat? What else?
How come no eggs?

How easy to invent the meal
I might have eaten, tell her I did.
But since I'm also the mother

of a grown child—
who negotiates these same
tight curves and steers so deftly—

I toast a slice of that 12-grain bread
she bought, which she doesn't like,
but I do, and lay on an extra-thick

slather of scallion cream cheese.

Savor

Some days, when I can barely
tell fried eggs from oatmeal,
how do I so clearly,
after 47 years, still taste the BLT
my boyfriend snacked on minutes
before we kissed in his mother's kitchen?
It's right here: that slippery sweetness,
tomato seeds stuck in his teeth.

After

Silhouettes of wet leaves stick to the road long after
the leaves themselves have clumped in the ditch.
It's the same with slug slime—no slugs there— and smudges
of woolly bears nicked by wheels passing.

I know the names of two of my four great-grandmothers,
Mintze and Gitl. Only their names, not the pitch
of their nagging, the smell of the soap they used to scrub floors,
how hard they slapped, which soups they liked best.

They're buried someplace or other. The ones who cried for
those deaths have been folded, too, into rich,
grub-riddled earth. Listen: tens of thousands of carved stones
slowly loosening, row on row of incisors and molars.

Stuff

Up close, it's thousands of granules—
emerald, ochre, rose—
the young monks paid out
from thin metal tubes, forming
gateways, divinities, flowers, fire.

The work took three days.
The instant they'd filled
in the last lines,
with no more pause than between
one breath and the next,

they picked up their brushes.
It doesn't take long to collapse
a world to a gray scrawl.
Half the sand they spooned
into zippered bags

stamped Mystical Arts of Tibet.
We stood in line to claim one each.
The rest went into an urn,
which they carried, chanting and
blowing those long horns—

dung chen—beating on drums.
At the bridge, one monk lifted
the urn to the top rail
and tipped it toward the creek.
The sand flashed as it fell.

So often since that day
I've come across this pouch
in my desk drawer, the contents
like stuff I'd slap from clothes
walking home from the beach.

Each time, I think
how a wiser person
would toss this packet, or empty it
into the breeze outside,
not tuck it back with the ballpoints

and Post-its, a near-empty vial
of Tabu, or this dented cap
from a Moxie bottle
one of the Davids I loved
in high school gave me and surely forgot.

I Take up Yarn Bombing

Because it's so difficult to love November's
ashes, streaked mud, cobwebs, husks.

Because I remember the small brown birds
going *chink, chink* like coins in the ivy all winter.

Because the kid with all the oil pastels
grew up and moved someplace warmer.

Because even after twenty-five years,
I regret letting go of that peacock mask.

Because nostalgia is a perilous elixir:
addictive, it makes the throat go numb.

Because the way to kill that desire
is to cap the bottle, swallow the spoon.

Because some women have the power
to turn parking meters into mermaids.

Because graffiti is the city's icy river—
drink it, or dive in and swim.

Because the road doesn't run forever,
but quick feet throw off rainbows.

Because what I need right now is
a thick, fruity syrup to pour on my fear.

Bereft

I lost the silver pendant
Malka gave me when I was eight.
Lost my grandmother's spoon
and great-grandfather's teapot
and cracked Jane's Japanese cup.

I lost Jon Cohen entirely—
eighth grade teacher,
sideburns, blue eyes, name
so common Google shrugs.

Mrs. B's print cotton robe,
a Christmas gift, I cut for dust cloths.
Ann's peasant blouse I've worn
down to patches and threads.
Now Ann's gone.

Monkees albums, guide to the World's Fair—
vanished. Also the ten or so chords
I learned on guitar.

I drop more Yiddish year by year,
and I must have misplaced my father,
my cat, the white dress,
the infant I nursed, the sticky toddler.

How many years till a swollen river
swallows the shoebox of mail,
the photos, cassette tapes, thumb drives,

and leaches the ink
from my twenty-six journals,
every loop and dot of this life
sipped off like so much vodka?

Aubade

Past sixty, long married,
I wake from a dream
in which a man
for whom I suffered
one-sided love

forty years ago
kisses my mouth again
and again, his fiancé gone
for a few hours,
couch pillows kicked to the floor.

A blade of daylight
slices the blinds.
The fluster of young,
brown curls on my face
lifts off like mist from snow.

Living

1

Too much to do, short on sleep, I start making up
stories of how I would die if I could choose:

head propped on pillows, linens starched and ironed,
comforters heaped on the bed, sun reflecting

off snow in the side yard, spilling through windows,
while down from the bedside radio floats that voice

like warm amaretto. He's reading poems,
bits of *Huck Finn,* the *Wall Street Journal,*

White Pages, what does it matter?
Eyes fall shut. Sleep trickles from cell to cell.

2

My father took five days to die,
head shaved and wrapped in gauze,

tube down his throat, machines pumping.
In the waiting room, I sat with maroon yarn

and needles I'd dug up somewhere.
Hour after hour. Each time a cousin or aunt

walked in, they asked, *What are you knitting?*
and each time someone cracked, *It's a* chuppah!

By the third day I'd given in: *Yep,*
you got that right, I'm making a chuppah.

3

This morning, R.—he's in his eighties,
taught me *Oedipus* and *Hamlet*, wasn't even

forty when I saw him last—writes, in an e-mail,
The cancer has moved to a place where there's no cure.

Now I'm sure it's time to dismantle the plastic
what-if Tinker Toy spools and sticks,

shake the Etch-a-Sketch back to its blank slate,
bang the door shut on the playroom,

surrender the corners to spiders, and start,
blight or not, on the job I was born for.

Harvest

The pepper plants
        Ed moved from the garden
                in white tubs, and hauled

indoors to live with
        the rest of our clutter,
                dropped all their leaves

by Thanksgiving. But now,
        with the ground hard,
                lawn still white,

they've slipped us flowers.
        One's even squeezed out
                a small fruit, gnarled

as a toothless gnome.
        We won't eat it.
                It's not food we're after,

just this off-kilter, out-of-
        proportion pleasure of seeing
                kinked, bare bones give birth.

Merrill Oliver Douglas grew up in Queens and spent some time in New Jersey and Manhattan before settling in upstate New York. She holds a B.A. from Sarah Lawrence College and an M.A. in English from Binghamton University. Earlier in her career, she worked in arts administration (including several years at The Academy of American Poets) and as a reporter and editor for a publisher of business newsletters. Since 2000, she has run a freelance writing business, where her clients include trade magazines, corporations, university publications and charitable foundations. Douglas's poems have appeared in *Baltimore Review, Barrow Street, Crab Creek Review, South 85 Journal, Tar River Poetry, Stone Canoe, Valparaiso Poetry Review, Paterson Literary Review,* the *Comstock Review, Sugar House Review* and other journals. She lives with her husband near Binghamton, N.Y.

www.ingramcontent.com/pod-product-compliance
Lightning Source LLC
LaVergne TN
LVHW041513070426
835507LV00012B/1531